JOKUMARASWAMI

A play in nine scenes

Chandrasekhar Kambar

Translated from the Kannada by
RAJIV TARANATH

Seagull Books

CALCUTTA 1989

SEAGULL BOOKS
A Publishing Programme for the
arts and media scene in India

Translation and introductory material
© Seagull Books, Calcutta 1989

Cover illustration by
Chittrovanu Mazumdar

Cover design by
Bashobi Tewari

ISBN 81 7046 034 4

*Performance rights in English controlled
by the author and the translator*

*Published and printed by Naveen Kishore,
Seagull Books, 26 Circus Avenue, Calcutta 700 017*

*Set by Neatpoint Photocomposers
Flat 20, 7 Chowringhee Road, Calcutta 700 013*

*Printed at Sun Lithographing Company
18 Hem Chandra Naskar Road, Calcutta 700 006*

Contents

A Note from the Publisher

Jokumaraswami by Chandrasekhar Kambar forms part of Seagull Books'
New Indian Playwrights series, which aims at building up a comprehensive
and representative series of new Indian plays covering the period from the
sixties downwards in the major languages—theatrically major—of the
country. In the next four years, all the significant new Indian playwrights
should be featuring on the Seagull list.

Playwrights appearing for the first time with Seagull Books will include
Mahesh Elkunchwar and Satish Alekar from Marathi, Kavalam Narayana
Panikkar from Malayalam and Ratan Thiyam from Manipur; while there
will be new titles by Badal Sircar, Vijay Tendulkar and Utpal Dutt who are
on our list already.

The first four pages of photographs are from the Benaka production of
1974. The remaining photographs are of the 1989 production done by
Ninasam, Heggodu. They are taken by P. S. Manjappa, Heggodu.

Introduction

An apparently wild opulence is what greets the reader as he delves into Kambar's writings. It is better that the reader relaxes into that opulence. For if he insists on taking a framework of logic into his reading then that very frame might trip him up.

In play after play the pivot is a fantasy or a superstition which has elements of a problem, and the play itself is the working out of the problem in, one notes, importantly man-woman terms and not husband-wife terms. Indeed, this could be described as a Kambar paradigm in which there is a shift from socially acceptable relationships into more powerful primordial bonds. It recurs in variation in *Jokumaraswami* as well as in *Siri Sampige, Kadu Kudure* and *Rishyashringa;* and is suggested in his poetry as well. The consequences are invariably painful. However, the tone always celebrates the primordial as against the local and the social 'mores.' Nowhere in Kambar do we find extra-marital love viewed pejoratively. The Gowdathi–Basanna pairing is the culmination of a logic very different from the routine logic of social propriety. Thus these consummations come through as experiences where the epiphanic joy of the couple neighbours with the menace of social propriety, hovering without in the form of ritual torture and death. In this shift from the social to the primitive, Kambar is placing instances side by side, and allowing endorsements and rejections to arise naturally.

It is obvious that Kambar's writing literally teems with images and symbols, and so, one could be tempted into discussing Kambar just in terms of symbolism. In fact there is something at once more simple, fresh and profound operating. Kambar builds with words which are pieces, stories or pictures, heard or felt dreams, all of which arise from his environment. Indeed, the manner in which he relates to his environment both in time and in space is through the stories, fantasies and images that he uses. It is not as if he is trying to relate in a poetic manner something which already exists: outside there is only anonymous stock, plural and characterless like bricks and mortar. In order to internalize it Kambar must build with it. And in this task he gives character to his environment and imbibes it again as a writer. They make each other.

He looks around and looks to himself. What he seems to find is always in terms of plenitude—mad joy, shimmering cruelty, pain, sex, loneliness, unbelievable quests by legend-like people in legend-like structures—all of which he celebrates. Celebration is, for Kambar, a primary mode of experience. And because the celebration has a musicality at once private and shared, the rhythm is at once private and contemporary, a blend of self and community. In celebrating, Kambar functions crucially as a myth-maker. To recognize him as a myth-maker is to make a crucial identification of the most significant configuration of Indian poetic genius. For among the major cultures of the world the Indian is perhaps the only one which continues to hold an easy transaction with the great and plural world of myth. The Sanatana mythogony is only a very small part of the dark and passionate world in which Kambar makes his space. Myth celebrates: philosophy contemplates. The mythical episteme is one of recognition as growth. The philosophical, is one of reduction of the many into one manifestation and the single essence. As a poet Kambar can only be plural and hence rich. Behind all the Upanishadic monism, India is mythical. Because we still bargain with our gods and walk among them and sometimes as them, our worship is essentially participatory, rituals in which men and their gods are parts of the same structure. In this, we Indians are a mythical people. To be a poet, Kambar must needs be mythical.

Kambar writes at a time when a version of western modernism is the presiding tone in Kannada literature. Indeed, some of his less important writings show a naive anxiety to be 'contemporary.' However, in his more important works he seems to question the validity of structures of western modernism as necessary to the writer's first task of relating to his environment. To Kambar the problem of being is more fundamental and universal. Modernism simply does not suffice. Kambar's work is a process of acceptance and transformation. Modernism is one of precise rejection.

The writer always deals with the sense of time and the sense of space. Kambar draws his texture of experience mainly from his sense of space, it forms the core of his writing. He is even a bit suspicious of an insistence on time, for time is abstract and could grow to be a neurosis in a writer. To a writer like Kambar, as to the painter and to the sculptor, place is the core of perception. Kambar certainly is of his time as unavoidably as he is of his place; but the relative emphasis decides the character of his writing, and keeps it apart from that of his peers in Kannada. Environment to him is the sense of place, ranging from the actual to the fantastic–mythical.

Kambar's insistent relationship with place also has something to do with his social background. He does not belong to an upper, or Sanskritized, caste. Hence, he is distant from the contrasts central to the upper caste inheritance: time–eternity, *Janma–Moksha,* appearance and essence and so on, all of which are dwelt on in the traditional Upanishadic culture. Not being burdened with these basically time-based structures, he is a child with a child's 'illiterate' fascination for powerful immediacies of sense. A true and easy sense of the many is his kind of relating: hence his inevitable kinship with myth-making.

In a sense, not belonging to the upper class has helped him enormously. His people, illiterate and oppressed, sang vividness in order to preserve experience. Sensuous memory was, in fact, all knowledge to them. And so when literacy and writing came to him, their son, it came as unique excitement, not as routine. Therefore, he builds. He does not, because he cannot, reduce and classify.

In this country, with its variety of social and intellectual structures, ranging from the heavily abstracting Sanatana to the non-reducing sensibility of the primitive and oppressed, it is possible to relate to one's environment with a power and variety unthinkable in the urbanized and anonymous social structure elsewhere. A mythical episteme is still valid, natural and real here. To say this is to point out the core of Kambar's importance to literature.

RAJIV TARANATH

Folk Theatre as I See It

I am often asked for my reading of what folk theatre is, its relevance to me, to my times and to my people.

Let me begin with myself. I belong geographically to a village, and sociologically to what was considered to be an oppressed, uneducated class. I am, therefore, a folk person simply because I honestly cannot be anything else. (I stress this point because in these last ten years a kind of 'folksiness' has become the 'in' thing with the sophisticated urban class.) The first long poem I wrote, *Helatena Kela* was entirely drawn from my soil. Looking at it twenty-five years later I find that most of my writing is thematically connected with that long poem. This is not a statement of a painful effort at thematic consistency; nor is it, I hope, a statement of creative bankruptcy. The sheer comprehensiveness and opulence of the experience as it formed itself in *Helatena Kela* has given me structures and approaches adequate to my most varied needs as an artist and as a man trying to articulate the creative urge of my people. I might make bold to state that the kind of folk medium which made *Helatena Kela* possible also made *Jokumaraswami* and other plays of mine possible. I have a feeling, which has endured these many years and will endure hereafter, that I am handling an art which is *total*.

I realize that my claim is bound to be controversial, especially as a statement coming from me towards the end of the twentieth century; and so I wish to discuss and elaborate the statement. To begin in a simple fashion, the calendar to me is not an important calibration of change in matters of sensibility. A people senses relevance of experience according to needs, imaginative and emotional, which are much more indirect and subtle. The durability or the transitoriness of experience and the art it engenders is something that occurs out of the socio-cultural needs of a people, their anguishes, their puzzlements and their exhilarations. The artist who draws his creativity strongly from his people articulates and places that sense of relevance. It is a fact that my people, even today, live governed largely by feudal values and have structures and textures of living which belong to other, previous, times. I am not being apologetic or critical. An artist uses fact as stuff and in doing so, might effect a very slight change in his people, in himself and in their relations. Sometimes, if he is fortunate, he might alight on structures, tones, myths and symbols which are so fundamental and hence so powerful, that issues like contemporaneity simply do not feature where he functions. For instance, I began by telling a story of fertility, impotence and drought in *Helatena Kela* and have continued to work around those themes in all my plays. T.S. Eliot and Yeats, both products of a western and largely urban culture, and prime spokesmen of literary modernism, nevertheless had similar themes at the centre of their oeuvres. Believe it or not, I draw my stuff from my village, not from Eliot or Yeats. What I mean to say is that there are aspects of the human condition so fundamental that they ever oppress, ever stimulate, and in this they lie under and beyond time and place.

There is another sense in which I want to look at the term 'total'. One might say that human society has passed through various stages or one might say that human society is found in various conditions. There is that society in which, for many reasons, the quality of living is one of sanctioned inhibition; of suppressed drives, emotional or sexual. The only area of living in which inhibitions are necessarily removed is the area related to religion. We find in such societies that a normally inhibited member breaks out of the restraining structures only in a situation which has religious sanction. Hence the phenomena of all kinds of frenzied behaviour associated with religious rituals in societies otherwise inhibited. And the frenzy includes superhuman feats and self-mortification, as well as sex. In short, these are necessary outlets for the survival and sanity of that society. Proceeding further we also observe that the distinction here between the realm of entertainment and the realm of actual living is as clear as that between normal living and participation in religious ritual. Paradoxically, it is because of this very definite separation that the realm of entertainment in such a society assumes a total and microcosmic character—microcosmic in the sense that entertainment then reflects all the creative urges and needs in the world outside. Thus it is at once a phenomenon both of concentration and comprehensiveness. And therefore the folk theatre includes dance, drama, narration, song, sex, death and religion. Most importantly, it is not only the actors who are separate from the world outside but the audience of the play as well. For the audience of the folk play *participates* in the play. Indeed, both the actors and the audience are co-participants in what is ultimately a shared religious ritual in the form of a play. The shoddiest production of a Bayalaata begins with prayer and ends with the audience as well as the players going to a temple, early in the morning. Against this background, clichéd remarks against song and dance in our plays are irrelevant. These remarks arise out of a different understanding of the function of entertainment, in societies different from the kind of societies I have described. In what might be called a modern society there is conscious and unconscious secularization: more and more of the important happenings in a man's life are detached from an overall religious framework. Simultaneously we see that the area of religious influence narrows and religion becomes almost a profession, functioning at certain socially sanctioned centres. Art, dance, drama, song, spread out into society at large, and in doing so, they also get separated from one another. A Londoner finds his dance, song, drama and religion at different places. A man from my village looks for all these things together. To simplify, Ibsen is impossible in my village; but, may I add, he should not be possible.

I shall try to explain this phenomenon in somewhat different terms. A criticism is often made, and not entirely without justification, that our plays, being full of action-retarding and theme-diluting music and dance and poetry, are escapist. While there might be some substance in this criticism when it relates to some of our secular plays and films, it cannot apply to our folk theatre. The entertainment in the folk theatre, it should be obvious by now, is importantly compensatory in nature. It is there that a man who lives a deprived existence in many ways under socio-cultural inhibitions, sees himself as full, and rising above the limitations of his deprived existence. And the religious framework in which this important release and completion takes place indicates a sanction which encompasses his micro as well as macro realms. On the other hand, the urbanite (my Londoner) has a choice between entertainment and religion, and in entertainment itself a choice of various kinds and levels. If he attends a musical or a strip show, his act is escapist. If there is music or the stripping of Draupadi in a Bayalaata, the import is different. It is fundamentally religious and compensatory. That the symptoms of escapism and the signals of a folk play appear similar is merely an accident of structural similarity. One has to think alertly to see the difference in import.

I am asked sometimes what I think about the future of folk theatre. Will it be valid in the coming world of computers and star wars? I am obliged to repeat what I have suggested before. Folk theatre, like language, is always adequate to the needs of its users at any given point in time. It will be valid as long as its users need it to be. If change occurs with the slow gradualness of history, it will survive into future times. If apocalyptic change occurs, it will not survive. But then, neither will its users.

CHANDRASEKHAR KAMBAR.

A Note on Jokumaraswami

Jokumaraswami is a phallic god and he is worshipped even today in the villages of north Karnataka. An annual festival which normally occurs in August-September, *Jokumara Hunnive* (full moon night), is named after him. The worship starts on the eighth day *(ashtami)* of the month of Bhadrapada. Women belonging to the castes of fisherman, washerman and lime-maker make phallus-shaped idols of Jokumaraswami out of wet clay. Applying butter to the phallus tip, they place the idols in baskets. Packing each idol firmly into an erect position with *neem* (margosa) leaves, they carry the baskets on their heads and go from house to house singing songs in praise of Jokumaraswami. Householders give them alms of salt, chillies and tamarind in response to the ritual begging.

In some villages the village boys get together and make a huge phallus eight to ten feet long, and tip it with lime. At its base, they stick hair gathered from a barber shop. It is believed that barren women become fertile if they sit on this phallus. In other villages, they cook snake-gourd as an embodiment of Jokumaraswami and feed it to the husbands of barren women.

Jokumaraswami is associated with rain. It is believed that even a rainless month will end with a shower on *Jokumara Hunnive*. There are many stories about Jokumaraswami in folklore. There is an ancient myth behind all these stories, a myth which is relevant to the play. It goes somewhat like this: Jokumaraswami, the son of Shiva, takes birth on earth as the son of Ditnadevi. From the second day after his birth till the sixth he seduces all the women of the village. On the seventh day the angry cuckolds of the village kill him with ritual cruelty. Wherever his blood falls, the earth turns green and fertile.

Jokumaraswami was first produced in the original Kannada by Pratima Nataka Ranga, at the open air theatre of Ravindra Kalakshetra, Bangalore, on 11 May 1972 with the following cast:

GOWDA	Girish Karnad
BASANNA	Umesh Rudra
GURYA	Krishna Raju
GOWDATHI	Sarada Umesh Rudra
NINGI	Revati
SHARI	Girija
BASSI	Kalpana
SHIVI	Asha
SERVANTS	1. Prasanna
	2. Arjuna
	3. Mohan Ram
	4. Gopalakrishna
SUTRADHARA	Chandrasekhar Kambar
HIMMELA	B. V. Karanth
MELA (CHORUS)	Siddharamaiah, Bharathi, Doddarange Gauda, Sunanda, Vijayalakshmi.
DIRECTION	B. V. Karanth
MUSIC	Chandrasekhar Kambar
STAGE DESIGN	V. Ramamurthy
COSTUMES	Prema Karanth

The Hindi version of this play was produced by Theatre Unit and Avishkar, directed by Satyadev Dubey, at the Prithvi Theatre, Bombay, on 20 June 1979. It was also produced and directed by Rajinder Nath at Shriram Centre for Art and Culture, New Delhi, on 17 March 1980.

Jokumaraswami has also been translated into and produced in Punjabi, Tamil and Gujarati. It has been performed at Calcutta, Chandigarh, Madras and Ahmedabad amongst other places.

Above The play begins with a song praising Jokumaraswami, led by Himmela
(B. V. Karanth) and Sutradhara (C.Kambar) on the extreme left and right respectively.
Below Basanna (Sunder Raj) confronts Gowda (Somasekhar Rao).

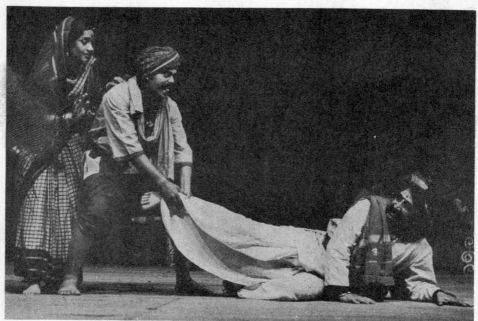

Above Ningi (Padmasri) taunts Gowda who receives a further blow to his prestige *(below)* at the hands of her mate, Gurya (Ramesh).

Above Deserted by her husband, Gowdathi mourns his indifference and decides to seduce him *(below)*, not realizing that she is speaking to Basanna.

Gowdathi yields to the irresistible Basanna.

The tables turn on tyrannical Gowda as Gurya, supported by Basanna *(above)* and Ningi *(below)* makes up for his earlier humiliation.

Above Basanna takes Gowda's henchmen by surprise, but this victory is shortlived.
Below He is eventually killed by a gang of men led by Gowda.

Ganna Pada
(Opening Prayer)

We salute you, O Lords and Masters !
Don't please disturb the play.

Young novices we are, frightened of paint,
Do attend well to our ballad.

Sit through it, O men and women,
And let the hall be full,
And let the love of wise men
Be upon us.

Lord Savalagi Shivalinga,
May your blessings be upon us.

Prologue

*At the centre of the stage, there is a basket filled with vegetables.
In the middle of this basket, a snake-gourd stands prominently.*

SUTRADHARA. Salutations to all of you, sitting or standing. Can you see this new god? His name is Jokumaraswami. Not that he is new to you. But there is a difference between him and other gods. The other gods grant a mouthful of boons the moment they are flattered a little. But somehow or the other, like the promises our ministers make, not one boon comes true. On the other hand, this god does not speak when he is flattered. But if you hold him in your arms after worship, he fills your lap with children. Indeed, the theme of this evening's play is the story of this unusual god. Who's there? Ho! Himmela!

HIMMELA. What? Why did you call me?

SUTRADHARA. Jokumaraswami must be worshipped before the commencement of our play. Please bring all the necessary ingredients and offer him worship according to the scriptures.

HIMMELA. Where did you say the god was?

SUTRADHARA. Can't you see him there?

HIMMELA. Ah, you mean this god !

SUTRADHARA. Why, what's wrong with this god?

HIMMELA. Instead of worshipping Ganesha at the commencement of the play, you want to worship this kind of god. Don't you understand? What will those who know think about us?

SUTRADHARA. You idiot ! When all gods are one and the same, what does it matter which god you worship? Come to think of it, this Jokumaraswami is the younger brother of Ganesha, and indeed today's play is about him. You shouldn't forget our original God.

HIMMELA. What's so great about Him?

SUTRADHARA. On this auspicious occasion, if barren women offer worship to this god, and afterwards make a curry out of him to feed their husbands, dozens of children will be born in a jiffy.

HIMMELA.	Quite right. And that's why a few women have come to the show. You don't seem to know anything about family planning at all.
SUTRADHARA.	My dear Himmela, if young women who have lost the love of their husbands only cook and feed this god to them, then all wayward husbands will begin to stick to their homes like ageing pet dogs.
HIMMELA.	I suppose many women don't know this.
SUTRADHARA.	Don't chatter anymore about such a god. Go fetch the ingredients for worship.
HIMMELA.	All right, all right. 'Bring' you order, so I'll bring them. But later if people scoff and scold, it's your look-out. Shall I bring the things?
SUTRADHARA.	Yes.
HIMMELA.	You are shameless. What shall I bring?
SUTRADHARA.	Holy grass, holy leaves.
HIMMELA.	Holy grass and leaves? Is your god some cow? Why don't you let him graze in a field?
SUTRADHARA.	You idiot! Don't talk lightly about a god who's like fire. Cleanse yourself and bring the holy leaves.
HIMMELA.	So be it, Sutradhara. Here are holy leaves and holy grass.
SUTRADHARA.	And get some rosewater also, all right?
HIMMELA.	Yes, I've understood.
SUTRADHARA.	What did you understand?
HIMMELA.	The water barbers use for shaving, isn't that rosewater?
SUTRADHARA.	You idiot! Purified water is called rosewater. Get that rosewater.
HIMMELA.	Yes. Here, I've brought it.
SUTRADHARA.	Get some flowers and fruits, and, to offer worship, a chaste woman.
HIMMELA.	Your god seems to be terribly expensive. I can bring flowers, I can bring fruit, but where will I find a pure, chaste woman? You're sure you want only a pure, chaste woman?
SUTRADHARA.	Yes, only a pure, chaste woman will do.
HIMMELA.	And if there's a little adulteration?
SUTRADHARA.	Shut up.
HIMMELA.	Sutradhara, I can get you fruit and flowers. But I can't manage this chaste woman business. There simply

isn't anyone of that sort these days. If you want, you can count me in as a chaste woman, and make do with me.

SUTRADHARA. Why, what's wrong? Why do you say this?

HIMMELA. Why? Will any self-respecting person come to worship such a god? In fact, if you want to know the truth, if you're looking for anyone at all chaste, you will find him amongst us four or five boys. Tell me, why is this god always after women?

SUTRADHARA. All right, you do the worship.

Sutradhara sings with the chorus, Mela, while Himmela performs the act of worship.

MELA. Come, my little Lord,
Come, my pretty moon,
Come, Jokumaraswami !
Lord of the green and Lord of abuse,
Lord of spicy offerings.
You fell as rain and sprouted as harvest,
And laughed young and fresh among the wild flowers.
You laid all the girls within two days of your birth.
And their men came chasing you with their sickles.

HIMMELA. How can you worship such an obscene god, especially in a public place?

SUTRADHARA. Such labels are for human beings. Among the gods, there's no 'clean' or 'obscene.'

HIMMELA. Do you know what you have forgotten at the moment?

SUTRADHARA. What?

HIMMELA. You have forgotten shame.

SUTRADHARA. If I hold on to shame my god will get angry. Listen quietly.

HIMMELA. Right, shoot !

MELA. Menstruating maidens you laid
On the third day after your birth,
And the uncles chased you
With axes and sticks.
The old women you pulled, Lord,
On the fourth day,
And the old men chased you
With rocks.

The wives you pulled, Lord,
On the fifth day
And their children chased you
With net and rope.
The widows you tugged,
On the sixth day
And they set
Five hundred on you.

HIMMELA. Given the slightest of chances you're in great voice
What do you think? Who doesn't know how to yell out
a song? Shall I? *(He sings.)*
You sat in a car and fell into the theatre.
Don't you have a home to sleep in?

SUTRADHARA. Why? Didn't I sing beautifully?

HIMMELA. Oh yes! Too beautifully. Do please sing a little less
beautifully. Otherwise the people gathered here might
understand you. The point is to sing it un-
understandably.

SUTRADHARA. All right. Shall I then describe the greatness of this god
in prose?

HIMMELA. Yes please. Or else this god is a big risk.

SUTRADHARA. In which case, listen. This our great god, the god
of green, of rains, of harvests, of abuses,
Jokumaraswami . . .

HIMMELA. Oho!

SUTRADHARA. Within two days of his birth, all the girls in the
town . . .

HIMMELA. Aha!

SUTRADHARA. He laid.

HIMMELA. You went wrong there.

SUTRADHARA. Why?

HIMMELA. What a rare creature this god of yours is! Only men
who're idle chase and lay women. And your god acts
like them. He laid girls, he laid hags, shouldn't you at
least be more prudent in your language?

SUTRADHARA. How?

HIMMELA. I mean, the term 'laid'. People here think it's obscene.
Do you see who is sitting in front? You really can't be
obscene in such a gathering. Shall I tell you a trick?
Instead of saying he 'laid' them, he 'laid' them, say he

'made love to them', he 'made love to them'.

SUTRADHARA. Righto! This our great god . . .

HIMMELA. . . . green god, that god, this god, etc. god . . . Proceed.

SUTRADHARA. You know what he did on the third day after his birth?

HIMMELA. What?

SUTRADHARA. All those who menstruated . . .

HIMMELA. Obscene again! Remove that word, and say girls who had 'come of age.'

SUTRADHARA. On the third day after his birth, all the girls who had come of age . . .

HIMMELA. . . . he made love to them.

SUTRADHARA. On the fourth day, all the hags . . .

HIMMELA. . . . made love . . .

SUTRADHARA. On the fifth day, the wives . . .

HIMMELA. . . . made love . . .

SUTRADHARA. On the sixth day, the widows . . .

HIMMELA. . . . made love. Sutradhara, are you cooking this up or is it true? Anyway, what happened then?

SUTRADHARA. And then, on the seventh day, the husbands of the wives came with axes. The old women's old men came with rocks, and the sons of widows came with ropes and nets. In all, five hundred of them. And where did they come to?

HIMMELA. They came to Jokumaraswami.

SUTRADHARA. And what did they do?

HIMMELA. Wait a moment. I think you should describe what happened in poetry. Prose might be a bit dangerous.

SUTRADHARA. If so, then listen. What did the five hundred do to Jokumaraswami?

HIMMELA. What?

MELA. Count, and they are five hundred.
Count, and the hands are a thousand
Which grip and chop the tender god.
A thousand hands. In each hand
A sickle or an axe,
Which slash to death the tender god.
Killed and thrown him,
They have slashed and thrown him,
And the flowing blood

Fills the river and the pond.
Where the blood falls, springs the sprout
And the shoot,
And all the earth is fresh, is green.

During the song untouchable Shari enters dancing and, after bowing, is about to carry away the sacred basket. Himmela notices her.

HIMMELA.	Not bad, your god. He's got a luscious customer. *(Running to her.)* Who art thou, beauteous damsel? Why hast thou come out of thy noble palace to this noble gathering? Art thou about to carry away this god? By what name art thou known ? Be good enough to tell.
SHARI.	What is this? You talk like a book.
HIMMELA.	Sutradhara, please come here. I can't manage.
SUTRADHARA.	Lady, who are you? What's your name? Tell us prettily.
SHARI.	Sutradhara, do I have to tell you?
SUTRADHARA.	Yes, you must.
SHARI.	Sutradhara, old men call me little girl, little girl. Small boys call me old woman, old woman. Gentlemen who are neither call me the untouchable whore Shari.
SUTRADHARA.	Lady, now we know that your name is Sharavva, and the people gathered here also know it. But why did you come here and why do you desire to carry away Jokumaraswami? Please do let us know.
SHARI.	Sutradhara, Jokumaraswami is a great god. He gives children to barren women, and husbands to maidens.
HIMMELA.	Yes, and he gives you clients.
SHARI.	I waited to see if some barren woman would carry away our god. None came. At least let me take him. As I get older, I get fewer clients. I could at least hold the few I have if I feed them with a curry made of my god.
HIMMELA.	So, it seems this god is really useful.
SUTRADHARA.	Sharavva, if that's the case, please take the god.

Shari picks up the basket.

HIMMELA.	Here, wait, wait. *(He runs to stand behind her in a traditional pose of bestowing a blessing.)* My son

Sutradhara, I'm pleased with your worship. I bless this
evening's play. Begin your play hereafter.

Sutradhara bows.

Musket God

MELA.   There is a Gowda in a certain place,
               And the Gowda is a rogue,
               And he wears a big paunch,
               And he struts about carrying a gun.
               Lord of the town and its boundary,
               Gold, silver and gold again,
               And pretty wench and girl,
               All, claims the Gowda, are his.
               The Gowda has a wife,
               Let's call her Gowdathi,
               A comely woman she is.
               Rapt, she watches
               The parrot flying.

*As the song ends Gowda enters grandly from amidst the audience,
followed by four men carrying a musket, who are dancing and
singing, 'This is our god, Dum Dum is his name.'*

SUTRADHARA.   O thou brave man who hast entered here along with
               this retinue, who art thou? What is thy name? Please
               narrate all prettily.

*Gowda looks at the four members of his retinue and gesturing to
them to answer the Sutradhara, he sits on a string bed. The four
men bring the musket, stand it in front of the Sutradhara and,
hanging a turban on its barrel, laugh among themselves.*

ONE.   If you want to know who this is . . .
ALL.   This is our god
               Dum Dum is his name.
SUTRADHARA.   Is his name Dum Dum? The audience is anxious—
               what does this god do? Please describe it in detail.
ONE.   He has a trigger and behind the trigger a bolt. The
               moment he takes aim, he jumps once. 'Dum!' and

that's the end. So great is our god.

ALL.   This is our god,
Dum Dum is his name.

TWO.   In a war, the soldiers shoot at corpses. But our god
fires only at healthy people. One day, he fired at a sick
man. Where was that?

THREE.   In the devil's field.

FOUR.   Yes, in the devil's field. And as he fired at the sick
man, our god didn't jump, didn't sing, didn't say
'Dum!' He didn't speak for three days altogether. So,
one day, twelve untouchable field labourers were stood
in a line and our god fired at them saying, 'Dum.' Can
you tell me what remained?

SUTRADHARA.   A dozen corpses !

TWO.   No! When others fire, there are corpses. When our
Dum Dum god fires, there's only ash and a whiff of
smoke. How can I praise our god!

ALL.   This is our god
Dum Dum is his name.

SUTRADHARA.   Yes, and what does your god look like?

THREE.   Our god Dum Dum has a big belly. He digests
anything. Fellows like you get the gripes after eating
two or three *rotis**. Our god can digest human flesh,
and he just loves chicks.

All.   This is our god
Dum Dum is his name.

GOWDA.   Hello, Sutradhara. Do you know who I am?

SUTRADHARA.   Sir, I now know who you are, and so do the socialists
gathered here. *(Pointing at Basanna who has entered
quietly in the meanwhile.)* Who's he ? And why does
he stand there?

ONE.   This is the food of our Dum Dum god.

TWO.   No. He's the lamb meant for our Dum Dum god.

THREE.   No. He's the milch cow of our god.

GOWDATHI *(entering from the wings).* Listen.

GOWDA.   Why do you come here in front of all these people? Go
in, I'll listen to you later.

---

* Unleavened bread.

FOUR *(pointing out the Gowdathi)*. That's the field of Dum Dum god.
Gowdathi goes in.

SUTRADHARA.	Doesn't this fellow have a name?
ONE.	I wonder.
BASANNA.	Basanna.

Gowda gets up immediately.

GOWDA. Basanna? Come, come Basanna. You all there, go away and come back later. Basanna, why do you keep standing outside? Come in, come in. Would you care for a smoke ?

(The four move to one side of the stage and Sutradhara joins Mela.)

I know you are very cut up about your father's death. You shouldn't think I'm not sad about it. What a lovely old man, your father. Every morning he used to come calling on me and borrow a *bidi* * from me. But what's to be done? The old man was very obstinate, and wouldn't listen to anybody. I myself told him, as to a parrot, not to sleep in that field, that there was a ghost there, the ghost of a woman who had seven children. Did he listen to me? No. He snubbed me, saying that even evil spirits are better than some human beings. And he went to the field. Next morning, when I went to meet him, there he was . . . Sit down. Don't keep standing. You shouldn't worry too much. You can stay in my house.

BASANNA. I know how my father died.

GOWDA. Not just you, the whole village knows. The earth of that field is very unkind. Why, only yesterday, Gurya's two lambs were lost there.

BASANNA. I know how my father died.

GOWDA. Are you crazy? You seem to suspect me. You know why? You've taken all this too much to heart. That's why. Come, have a smoke and you'll feel better.

BASANNA. Gowda, let me tell you something loud and clear. I know how my father died. I know how he carved a field from out of a forest. I know how I shall never give up

---

* A popular, inexpensive 'cigarette' made of rolled leaf and tobacco.

GOWDA.	that field. Since you know so much, do you also know that your father had borrowed money?
BASANNA.	Whichever way you look at it, it was only 200 rupees. For twenty years, he gave you half his produce every year, and the loan is still not repaid?
GOWDA.	Let that pass. Do you know in whose name that field is registered?
BASANNA.	I don't know all that; the field is mine, and I'm going to plough it. If you have anything more to say, tell it to my back.
GOWDA.	In that case, I don't understand what you say. Say all that to my gun.

Basanna kicks the gun and goes away. Gowdathi enters and speaks after Basanna has left.

GOWDATHI.	Please listen!

The servants approach when they see Gurya coming from a distance. Gowdathi goes in.

ONE.	My Lord, Gurya has come and is waiting outside.
GOWDA.	Bring him in. *(Gurya comes in, frightened.)* Come, Gurya . . . This lamb is frightened, go away, you.

The four servants move away.

GURYA.	My Lord, two of my lambs were killed and eaten by the servants.
GOWDA.	Whose servants?
GURYA.	Your servants, the ones standing there.
GOWDA.	You bastard, you wag your tongue too much. Why did you allow your sheep to graze there? Didn't you let them graze in the devil's field?
GURYA.	Yes.
GOWDA.	You let them graze there, and the devil killed them. And you have the cheek to blame my servants. You bastard! The devil broke even a man like Basanna's father, will it leave your sheep alone? To add to this, you spread the scandal throughout the village. If anything dies in the village, it is said that Gowda or his servants are responsible. Bastards! You don't seem

	to appreciate the value of a Gowda. Wait a moment and I'll tell you who killed . . . *(He takes up the gun.)*
GURYA.	Not me, sir! Basanna said all this.
GOWDA.	Basanna? Tell me the truth. Why have you come here?
GURYA *(not knowing what to say)*.	Nothing special, my Lord, I came here . . . to press your feet.
GOWDA.	Well press them, then.

Gurya starts pressing Gowda's feet, in great fear.

GOWDA.	Gurya, you bastard, do you know who I am?
GURYA.	You are the Gowda of the village.
GOWDA.	Do you know who you are?
GURYA.	Your slave, my Lord.
GOWDA.	Are you frightened?
GURYA.	No, my Lord.
GOWDA.	Are you afraid of Basanna?
GURYA.	No, my Lord.
GOWDA.	Not frightened of me or of Basanna? You've become quite a politician.
GURYA.	I'm frightened only of you.
GOWDA.	If you fear me, then why did you go to Basanna? Bark!
GURYA.	I'll bark, my Lord.
GOWDA.	Why did you go to Basanna?
GURYA.	I didn't.
GOWDA.	He came to you?
GURYA.	Yes.
GOWDA.	What did you say? What did he say? Tell me everything properly, or else, you bastard, I'll skin you alive.
GURYA.	Basanna said, 'Gurya, I hear you've sold your field to the Gowda?' I said, 'No, we owed Gowda some money. He took the field in part repayment.' Basanna said, 'How much?' I said, ' 300.' He said, 'How could you sell him five acres for a mere 300 rupees?' I said, 'I don't know.'
GOWDA.	You son of a dog, you don't know? How long is it since I gave you 300 rupees?
GURYA.	Three or four years.

GOWDA.	Three or four years? Shall I get the papers? Ten years. Ten.
GURYA.	I was a small child then.
GOWDA.	When you were young, did you eat rice or cowdung? Do the documents lie? Does your thumb print lie? Didn't you take the money at the Durgavva's fair on Amavasya?
GURYA.	Yes, it was on Amavasya night.

The four servants in the background stand up and move closer.

GOWDA.	How long is it since that Amavasya?
GURYA.	Ten years.
GOWDA.	What is the total of the principal and the interest for ten years?
GURYA.	Five acres, my Lord.

The four move away again.

GOWDA.	It is ten, not five. Bastard! I've let you keep on working for me only because I pity you. Isn't there any value for a Gowda who rules the earth? If I so wish, I can make not only you but even Basanna eat dirt, understand?
GURYA.	Yes, I understand.
GOWDA.	Gurya, what do you understand?
GURYA.	That he'll eat dirt.
GOWDA.	Go tell Basanna his father hasn't given me last year's share. He's not to step into the field without repaying the loan.
GURYA.	All right.
GOWDA.	When will you go?
GURYA.	Right now, sir.
GOWDA.	Press my feet now. Go later.

Shivi and Bassi enter, but go inside hurriedly when they see Gowda. Then Ningi enters and removes her slippers.

GOWDA.	Who is this bird, Gurya? Hey you, stop! *(Ningi covers her face with her sari and stops.)* Whose daughter are you?
GURYA.	She is Gurupada's daughter.
GOWDA.	She's come of age, see how ripe she is. Isn't she

married yet?

GURYA. Not yet, sir.

GOWDA. What's your name, girl?

GURYA. Gowda is asking you, tell him. When Gowda himself wants to know your name why don't you reply?

GOWDA. Maybe she is scared! What a mouth-watering bit of a girl she is! Are you scared?

NINGI *(letting her sari slip)*. You are not a tiger or a bear for me to be scared of. I'm not panting with my tongue out just because the village Gowda asked my name . . . yaah . . .

She sticks her tongue out at him.

GOWDA. You crazy girl, who do you think you're speaking to? Can't you see clearly?

NINGI. Of course I can. The sun is shining and I have two eyes. Shall I say it? This is Gowda's face, these are my slippers.

She prepares to leave.

GOWDA. Stop, girl. Tell your father this. Tell him that I haven't left any land in this village untouched.

NINGI. There's plenty of land in this village where even the sun's rays haven't fallen. Understand?

She exits quickly.

GOWDA. To come to my place and give me such cheek! The chick has flown away. Gurya . . .

GURYA. Sir?

GOWDA. Will you marry her?

GURYA. Sir . . .

GOWDA. Will you marry her?

GURYA. Heh, heh, heh . . .

GOWDA. I'll sell her for three rupees. Will you buy?

GURYA. Heh, heh, heh . . .

GOWDA. Go cook a curry with plenty of spice. You eat it in my name, if you can't give it to me. What do you say?

GURYA. Heh, heh, heh . . .

GOWDA. Stop cackling, you bastard. Which girl will fall for a cur like you? How old are you?

GURYA.	Twenty-five.
GOWDA.	Have you ever seen a woman's thighs?
GURYA.	No, sir.
GOWDA.	How can you understand? Gurya, I want to catch this jungle fowl.
GURYA.	I know how to catch one, my Lord.
GOWDA.	Really? Tell me how.
GURYA.	You should place a cockerel in a cage. You should hang the cage in the forest. And when you crow like a cock, ko ko ko, wild hens will turn up. Shoot them.
GOWDA.	At least you know this much.
GURYA.	But even when a true cock like you crowed, the bird slipped away.
GOWDA.	Shut up, you bastard. Come here. Hold your ears. *(Gurya does as he says.)* Sit down, get up, down, up . . . Press my leg. *(Gurya starts pressing his leg.)* Gurya, to whom do the villagers pay more respect? To me or to Basanna?
GURYA.	To you, sir.
GOWDA.	Who are they more scared of?
GURYA.	You, sir.
GOWDA.	Say it properly.
GURYA.	The men are scared of you, the women are scared of Basanna.
GOWDA.	Really? Which woman has not been touched by Basanna?
GURYA.	The one who was here just now.
GOWDA.	Oh? What does she call Basanna ?
GURYA.	She calls him brother.
GOWDA.	Is that so ? She'll call me uncle. Tell Gurupada . . .
GURYA.	Yes sir . . .
GOWDA.	What'll you tell him?
GURYA.	I'll tell him that Gowda is hungry, give him your bird to eat.
GOWDA.	Go. I'll follow you shortly.

Gurya goes. Gowdathi comes in when Gowda is picking up the gun.

GOWDATHI.	What, are you going somewhere?
GOWDA.	You have the nerve to ask me ! Haven't I told you not to ask where and why I'm going out?

GOWDATHI.	Will you at least come home tonight?
GOWDA.	She is as worried as if she can't bear to part from me. Finish telling me whatever you want to say while I smoke a *bidi*. I'll listen. *(He lights up.)*
GOWDATHI.	Tonight is Jokumara's full moon night. It has been ten years since we got married.
GOWDA.	So?
GOWDATHI.	On that day the full moon was so big.
GOWDA.	So it was.
GOWDATHI.	On that day, my mother said that by next Jokumara full moon night, a little male child would be playing in our house.
GOWDA.	Really? I don't remember.
GOWDATHI.	I had a dream last night.
GOWDA.	Did you ? What did you dream?
GOWDATHI.	There was a full moon. A rainbow coloured parrot was sitting on a tree in our garden. Even in the moonlight its colours were shining. Then, for some reason, everyone started laughing. Up there our moon was growing smaller and smaller like a rusted coin . . . Why have you neglected me so much?
GOWDA.	Either you are still sleepy, or you must have fever. I've told you not to worry too much. If I worried like you I wouldn't have so much hair left on my head.
GOWDATHI.	How can you understand a woman's need?
GOWDA.	Come on, then, make me understand. Here, I'll light another *bidi*. Tell me.
GOWDATHI.	As if you really care for what I say. There was an old man hiding behind that small moon, taking aim at the parrot . . .
GOWDA.	You're still dreaming. Wake up.
GOWDATHI.	We've been married for ten years. Have I ever asked you a favour?
GOWDA.	What do you lack? First tell me that.
GOWDATHI.	I have everything! Food to eat, clothes to wear . . . Do you know what Gurupada's daughter said?
GOWDA.	What?
GOWDATHI.	'You have a field as big as the forest, a house as big as the village, but there is no child in the house.'
GOWDA.	Did she say that? Must do something about it.

GOWDATHI.	You said the same thing when we got married !
GOWDA.	Really? I don't remember. Tell her I won't forget this time.
GOWDATHI.	Tonight is Jokumaraswami's full moon night. I believe that if we worship Jokumaraswami and then cook and eat him, we will have children. So please come home for dinner.
GOWDA.	Oho! So that's why the ladies are here?
GOWDATHI.	Yes.
GOWDA.	Has Gurupada's daughter also come for the same reason?
GOWDATHI.	Yes. It seems you said something to her and she went home.
GOWDA.	Yes. What did you say her name was?
GOWDATHI.	Ningi.
GOWDA.	OK. So I'll come home for dinner this evening.
GOWDATHI.	Will you see if you can get a parrot?
GOWDA.	Will you do one thing ?
GOWDATHI.	Why one? Give me ten things to do.
GOWDA.	Not ten, one is enough. Will you do it?
GOWDATHI.	Tell me what.
GOWDA.	Will you shut up and go inside?

He goes out. Mela sings,'This is our god, Dum Dum is his name.'

Rise and Come, Beloved Parrot

MELA *(sings).*   Rise and come to us, beloved parrot, relishing the eastern breeze and filled with moonlight.

Bring to the parched earth the season of blossoming flowers, O, bird of distant lands.

Hearts are filled with sand, nests droop from the gaunt tree, the young in the womb cry, disconsolate even early in the night.

Anxious I stand. Come.

Gowdathi is on the verandah. Bassi is in the kitchen inside. Bassi speaks from within.

GOWDATHI.	Bassi . . .
BASSI.	I'm coming, ma'am.
GOWDATHI.	Come quick . . .
BASSI.	I just have to wipe my hands.
GOWDATHI.	You still have to sweep the floor and wash the threshold.

BASSI *(comes out)*. Have you had a bath?

GOWDATHI.	Doesn't it look as if I've had one? Whatever I do, it's the same. I feel thirsty from head to toe. Everything should be ready before Gowda returns. What have you told Shivi?
BASSI.	I've asked her to get Jokumaraswami from Sutradhara's basket.

During the following conversation, Bassi sweeps, draws auspicious patterns on the floor and lights the oven. Gowdathi helps her now and then.

GOWDATHI.	Bassi . . .
BASSI.	Yes, ma'am.
GOWDATHI.	Will I have children if this worship is done properly?
BASSI.	Would I lie, ma'am? Do you know that Deviri down the road?
GOWDATHI.	The one who got married on the same day as I did?
BASSI.	The same Deviri.
GOWDATHI.	But she has children.
BASSI.	That's right, and it's a long story. She didn't have children for a long time, like you. Her husband was ready to marry again. They even saw some prospective brides. One day Deviri was crying into her sari in the fields. 'Why are you crying?' I asked her. 'What can I say? My husband wants to marry again. God hasn't given me any children,' she said. Whatever you may say ma'am, don't I know who is barren and who is a mother? She smelt like a newly ploughed field even at a distance.
GOWDATHI.	There's a season to everything. It's not right to cross its limit.
BASSI.	Gowda's conduct is just not right. What's the use of having fields all round the village? Who will he leave it all to when he dies? Is he bothered? A young woman

	like you is sitting at home worrying about it, and he'd rather see a prostitute's thighs than his wife's face.
GOWDATHI.	It's all fate.
BASSI.	Ma'am. Why do you make me say these things? If the balls don't bless, what can God's blessings do? It needs a strong man to fulfil a woman. It's not enough to boast and threaten. Look at my husband. Years since we married, and he hasn't thrashed me even once. Still, if I see him coming I start trembling like a creeper in the breeze. It's true, ma'am, even old hags conceive if they so much as cross my husband's piss.
GOWDATHI.	It's all the grace of God. I prayed to God and he has thrown a broom in my lap.
BASSI.	Why do you upset yourself so? My name is not Bassi if this worship misfires.
GOWDATHI.	By the way, what did you tell Deviri?
BASSI.	Oh yes ! Deviri was crying—I asked her why. She said, 'What can I say? My husband is bringing home another wife.' 'Why is he bringing another wife?' 'Because I'm barren,' she said, and started weeping again. And yet, if men approach Deviri, her eyes start dancing like a leaf on a creeper. I've seen this myself. How can I believe that she's barren?
GOWDATHI.	I have told him so many times that this house needs children. He says, 'You're tired, go and rest.' Even other children are scared to come here. The other day, I offered them sweets. But did even one wretched child so much as turn this way? I wept inside when I saw them running away. 'What is this woman's life, God?' I cried. How can my cry reach God? His heart must be made of stone.
BASSI.	Look here, ma'am. Call me a wretch if you want, but a home should be lively with the sound of children and children should be weeping and their mother should be threatening them with the very devil. How charming it all sounds! And here? At night this house has only one lamp flickering, as if about to be put out any minute. There don't seem to be people in the house at all, and if there are, they speak in whispers.
GOWDATHI.	What did you tell Deviri?

BASSI.	I told her not to worry and to worship Jokumaraswami. She worshipped him, cooked him and fed him to her husband. The moment he ate that he started chasing Deviri like one demented. He was always inside her. Do you know what happened next? A child on Wednesday, a child on Saturday. It was as easy as laying eggs!
GOWDATHI.	So even she got children from Jokumaraswami?
BASSI.	Jokumaraswami is not a god to be taken lightly, ma'am.
GOWDATHI.	Bassi, does anyone here have a pet parrot?
BASSI.	Hah! A parrot. Do you know Basanna? He has a parrot, a very beautiful one. It doesn't fly away even if it's let out of its cage— it's always on his shoulder.
GOWDATHI.	Really?
BASSI.	Ma'am, he's even taught it to speak. It lisps so adorably!
GOWDATHI.	Is that really true?
BASSI.	It's true all right. All the village girls speak to it when they go to collect water.

Shivi enters.

SHIVI.	Ma'am, everything is ruined.
GOWDATHI.	Why?
SHIVI.	That prostitute Shari beat us to it. She's taken Jokumaraswami from Sutradhara.
GOWDATHI.	Then why didn't you go to her place?
SHIVI.	How can I go to where the untouchables live?
GOWDATHI.	For my sake, go. How can I spend another year mumbling God's name in vain? Go, and I'll give you loads of gifts.
SHIVI.	How can a respectably married woman go to a whore's house, ma'am?
GOWDATHI.	Right. As they say, you can't go to heaven unless you yourself die. Stay here, I'll be back.

Music. Gowdathi exits.

Bird of the Season

Gowdathi enters, sweeping the verandah of the whore Shari's house with the end of her sari.

GOWDATHI.   Beloved whore,
Whore, my mother,
Are you home?
Barren I come
To entreat you.
Pity you have none.
With my sari end
I sweep your front yard.
I stand, my lap barren.
Come out, I beg you,
And meet me.

SHARI.   Who are you, sweeping the verandah of a whore's house?
Who are you, O friend,
Why have you come?
Why do you sweep?
A rich family, a virtuous one,
You seem to belong to.
Why do you, O well-married one,
Come to a mere whore's yard?
Madam, you appear to be well-married and beautiful.
Who are you? Kindly be so good as to tell me.

GOWDATHI.   Mother . . .

SHARI.   You should call a low whore like me 'bitch', not 'mother'. Who may you be?

GOWDATHI.   Like you, I'm a woman.

SHARI.   I know that. I could call you an elder or younger sister. You look married. Tell me your name.

GOWDATHI.   The bird of the season has come and sat in your house. I'll tell you my name if you give me that bird.

SHARI.   Why, madam, do you talk in riddles? Why do you tire me out without giving me your name? What and where is this bird of the season?

GOWDATHI.   You have it at home and yet you ask me where it is.

SHARI.   Don't kill me with riddles. My house is blessed by your

	coming. Tell me your name and why you are here.
GOWDATHI.	Mother, I'll tell you my name if you give me Jokumaraswami.
SHARI.	What rival are you,

What rival are you,
What whore are you?
Want me to die, do you?
To the grave should I go,
No food, no water,
Not even a client !
I sit here waiting
And you pretend
To sweep my yard.
What whore are you,
What rival are you?
Of Jokumaraswami I wanted to
Cook a dish
And feed all the town males
And hold them in my sari
And lay them at my threshold
And you come to sweep my yard.
What rival are you,
What whore are you?
Twenty years have passed
Since I a whore became—
Nothing earned, nothing saved.
I thought that by the mercy of
Jokumaraswami I could purchase
Rope to hang my wretched self !
And you come to sweep my yard.
What rival are you,
What whore are you?
Which town whore,
Which lane whore?

GOWDATHI.   Mother,
Spreading my sari I beg,
Your feet I clasp,
Show me mercy!

SHARI.   You fool, which female will let go of Jokumaraswami?
I'm getting old. I don't have a daughter like you to look
after me. This body of mine has never slept without

	perfumed oil in its hair and a lover by its side. Now I've got a spell to bring all the lovers to me. How can I give that to you? No, I won't.

GOWDATHI.   Do not, I beg of you,
             Refuse me.
             As your daughter,
             Fill my lap.
             Spreading my sari I beg,
             Your feet I clasp,
             Show me mercy.

SHARI.   If I had a soft heart, would I be a whore? How can I give away such a stroke of luck to some wayfarer?

GOWDATHI.   Wretched and barren,
             I do entreat,
             Spreading my sari I beg,
             Your feet I clasp,
             Show me mercy.

SHARI.   I feel sad that you are barren. But what can I do? How can I let go of the good fortune in my hands? Go, after telling me your name.

GOWDATHI.   The wife of the Gowda.
             I am Gowdathi.
             Still I implore,
             Show me mercy.

SHARI.   The village Gowdathi? How can you be so mad, madam? You put aside your status and come to a whore's house, begging! Have you been married long?

GOWDATHI.   It is ten years today since I married.

SHARI.   Don't you know Gowda's weakness yet? Even if I give you Jokumaraswami how can you get children from Gowda?

GOWDATHI.   Why not? So many have borne children to Jokumaraswami!

SHARI.   Yes, others may have, but you still don't know Gowda's nature. Except for a vain desire to claim everything in this world as his, what else does he have? Look at me. I've spent a lifetime rubbing myself against hot men. Shall I tell you my experience? Look at Basanna. Any girl he looks at gets wet. He makes them wet even in their dreams. But the same girls have a hard time hiding their giggles when they see Gowda. Can such a fellow have children? On the day I had my first period Gowda came to ceremonially break my seal. He gave me a bag of rice, a sari, a blouse and five rupees. What wouldn't a young whore give to have Gowda as her first client? When I entered the bedroom with my sari loosened . . . Gowda was snoring. I spent the night pressing his feet. He went away in the morning as if nothing had happened. Since that day he has broken the seals of ten or fifteen girl whores and when you ask them how, they say what I've just said. You know why he did this?

GOWDATHI.   He must've felt bad about coming to a whore-house.

SHARI.   Everyday you press his feet and scrub his back in the bath. You have seen his front and you have seen his back and you still insist on loving him. You are a proper wife indeed. Do you know why he did what he did ? Whether he lay with them or not, the children of all the whores whose seals he was supposed to have broken would be counted as his children. So Gowda addresses anybody in the village as 'son of mine' . . . Can such a Gowda give you children?

GOWDATHI.   Why not, with the blessings of Jokumaraswami?

SHARI.   Do please take Jokumaraswami! But now that you have stood at the threshold of a whore's house at least learn to have your wits about you.

GOWDATHI.   Mother, how can I ever repay this great favour? Just bless me by saying once that I'll have children.

SHARI.   Go, you'll have children.

She puts the basket containing Jokumaraswami on Gowdathi's head. Gowdathi leaves. Music.

The Paunch Fell Down

Basanna and Gurya meet in the street.

BASANNA.   Friend Guranna, Ram Ram.
GURYA.   Friend Basanna, Ram Ram.

BASANNA.	Friend Guranna, why is your face downcast?
GURYA.	Friend Basanna, what can I tell you? I don't know if poverty is a curse; but it certainly isn't a boon.
BASANNA.	Why, my friend? I've never heard you talk with such pain. Tell me what's wrong.
GURYA.	Friend, the Gowda caught me today. He somehow came to know that I had met you and he wanted to ripen my backside with his kicks.
BASANNA.	If you're such a coward, who won't kick you? Has he swallowed your field?
GURYA.	Where is the question of swallowing? It seems that the field is now registered in his name. Gowda has a large belly and because he always speaks from inside that belly, what we say it can't hear, because it has no ears.
BASANNA.	What a fool you are! To let a field slip away in front of your eyes. Go tell him that there are new rules and regulations.
GURYA.	Debtors are always dumb.
BASANNA.	Don't worry. Let me see how he takes away your field.
GURYA.	You know what happened today, Basanna? Gowda set eyes on Gurupada's daughter Ningi, and didn't he get very, very hot ! You know what Ningi did?
BASANNA.	What did she do, my friend?
GURYA.	She spat on him three times and went away.
BASANNA.	That's how one should be.
GURYA.	I feel very brave when Ningi is close by.
BASANNA.	You want to marry her?
MELA.	This is our god. Dum Dum is his name

Gowda and his retinue of four enter.

GOWDA.	What, Gurya, you're still standing here! By the way, who's this fellow? What's his name? I seem to have seen him somewhere.
BASANNA.	You want my name? Shall I say it in riddles or just straight out?
ONE.	He is Basanna.

GOWDA *(shuts him up and tells all four to stand in a corner).* Oh! So this is Basanna. Gurya, did you tell him what I told you?

GURYA.   Sir, I haven't, but I will. Basanna, it seems your father
                hasn't given Gowda his share from the devil's field.

BASANNA.   What field? What talk is this? Haven't you shat well
                this morning? Why do you blabber? There is a law by
                which the field belongs to the one who ploughs it. Tell
                him that.

GOWDA.   Well, well, a great lawyer. It seems you have taken up
                Gurya's brief. Then you must see that he wins.

BASANNA.   You don't have to tell me that.

GOWDA.   Know this, all of you are living because of me.

ALL FOUR.   Yes, yes, sir, yes sir.

BASANNA.   Yes, yes, my Lord; we all live because of your mercy,
                don't we ?

GOWDA.   Shall I show you by whose mercy you live? Gurya . . .

GURYA.   Sir?

GOWDA.   Bend a little. *(Gurya bends and Gowda sits on him.)* By
                whose mercy do you live?

GURYA.   My Lord, by yours.

GOWDA.   Tell him that.

GURYA.   Basanna, I live by Gowda's mercy.

BASANNA.   Ho, ho, ho, ho! Yes, yes, Gowda, in the beginning even
                God used to say the same things. 'Children, you are all
                living because of my mercy.' But the other day, even
                the gods inside the temple were stolen, did you know
                that?

GOWDA.   The thieves' arses will itch. What will they do then ?

BASANNA.   Impossible.

GOWDA.   Impossible? Wait, I'll show you too. As from today,
                the field you plough is mine. Know that if you even
                step on that field hereafter, your legs will not be yours.

BASANNA.   Gowda, shall I tell you something?

GOWDA.   Tell it to this gun. I've taught it to speak. Do you hear
                what it says?

ALL FOUR.   Dum Dum.

BASANNA.   I also have a gun, but the ones I shoot at don't die, they
                litter. *(Laughs.)* Ningi was telling me that you have
                grey hair. Do you, Gowda?

GOWDA.   Shall I show you ? Here, get the gun. *(He takes the gun
                and Basanna puts his ear to the muzzle.)*

BASANNA.   Let me hear what it says . . . I can't hear anything. *(He*

| | *snatches the gun and throws it away.)* Get lost, you jabbering braggart. So you'll break my legs if I step into the field. Indeed ! Aren't you worried about your own legs? With aching arms, and starving bellies, my father and I cleared the forest. When men feared to pass that way even during the day, frightened of the devil's field, my father and I laboured there day and night! And now this fellow comes along and claims the field as his! |

GOWDA. Gowdaship is ours for generations. Your father has written off this field to us and has pressed his thumb at the bottom. You've come along now to change it all? Let laws and rules be made! In the end, the moneyed man is always the big man. I only have to throw six, if not three, coins and your laws and rules fall into my pocket. . . . I'll give you four rupees. Will you carry my gun ?

BASANNA. Well, well, you talk like a real hero. Even big kings have set up barber shops, but you haven't given up your arrogance. Shall I show you my hand ? *(Sitting in front of Gurya.)* Gurya, get up! Come what may, I'm behind you. Get up !

GOWDA. Doesn't a dog know whose dog it is? Doesn't it?

ALL FOUR. It does, it does.

ONE. Some curs, my lord, don't remember whose house they belong to. They hang around anyone who throws them crumbs.

BASANNA. Look, do you want to be a cur in his house? I'm like a tiger, I'm here to take care of you.

ONE. How many tigers has our Dum Dum god killed?

TWO. Eleven.

THREE. Not even a dozen?

BASANNA. Gurya, get up. Even Ningi, a young girl, could stand up to Gowda and a man like you lies prone? Up!

Gurya gets up at once. Gowda falls off. The four servants stand fixed in amazement while Mela sings. Gurya begins to dance in time to the song.

MELA. The paunch fell and tumbled
On the ground.
Floating eyes, frightened eyes,

And all that mud on the whiskers!
The paunched dog sat on the back
And claimed the world as his.
He tripped and stumbled
Bang! Flat on his back.

As the song ends, the four servants lift up the Gowda. One takes Gurya's prone position and when Gowda sits on him, the others comfort him.

GOWDA. Shameless dogs. If I leave you a little free because you are poor, you climb on my head. Gurya, will you come this side?

BASANNA. Watch how the Gowda picks up courage when his dogs are around him.

GOWDA. Who is this? A fly? Here you, talk to him.

ONE. Basanna, even before the lime on your father's stone is fully dried, are you tired of living?

BASANNA. Yes, I'm so tired that I'm waiting to be killed by a brave warrior like you. Why just me? That goes for all the poor of this village.

GOWDA. I allowed this unclaimed cur to go begging in the streets and now look at its arrogance!

BASANNA. Gowda, kindly count the teeth in your mouth before you talk.

GOWDA. I stay my hand because you're young, and you challenge me? Thrash him!

The four attack Basanna. Gurya runs, screaming.

GURYA. Aiyo! Cqme! Gowda is killing Basanna.

GOWDA. Hey, you fellows, get back. Gurya is gathering a crowd.

The four fall back. Basanna does a push up.

BASANNA. If you're a real man, don't send your dogs, come yourself. Try your arm against mine, and know my strength. Do you think it's as easy as killing my father?

GOWDA. Why all this male talk? Shall I set you a challenge, man to man?

BASANNA. Tell me.

GOWDA *(taking out betel leaves and nuts from his pocket)*. Let it be clear once and for all whose this field is, yours or mine. Let me be clear about it, you be clear, let the people be clear. Tonight is Jokumaraswami full moon night. Whoever can sleep through tonight in the field takes the field. Are you ready ? If so, take this betel.

ONE. Look, the devils are many on a full moon night. Basanna, remember where exactly your father died before accepting the betel.

TWO. Don't you know the story of that mother of seven children?

BASANNA. I'm ready, give me the betel. *(Exits.)*

GOWDA *(calls one of the servants).* You, go to my house. Get food and a blanket. If they ask, tell them at home that Gowda will sleep in the devil's field tonight. All of you go to that field and finish the job. You can eat the food meant for me. Come and tell me later what happened. I'll be at Shari's house, understand?

ONE. Yes sir.

Jokumaraswami

Gowda's house. Bassi, Shivi and Ningi are waiting for Gowdathi. Gowdathi enters with Jokumaraswami in the basket.

GOWDATHI. Bassi, how you frightened me needlessly! Shari gave it to me herself, no trouble at all! Start the worship quickly.

BASSI. Everything is ready.

Bassi, Shivi and Ningi start singing. They draw eyes and a moustache on Jokumaraswami, a snake-gourd, and wrap a turban around it. Gowdathi mimes parts of the song. The rest of them dance with her.

BASSI, SHARI AND NINGI.
A pretty green shirt,
A *dhoti* * of silk,
His turban at a jaunty slant—
Friend, let us worship Jokumaraswami,
Handsome Jokumaraswami!
What laughter under the moustache,

---

* A man's lower garment.

What brightness in the cheeks.
The naughty one with his brows
Ogles at the waists of flighty girls.
Isn't he Jokumaraswami?
At a hand clap he turns and glares,
Not we, but the barren ones have called you.
They await you, hands on brows—
Go kindly to them.
In their bosoms they'll hide you,
In flowers will they cover you.
Grant them fruits, great Lord—
That all-high God Jokumaraswami
Do we worship.

BASSI.   Now you should cook the god quickly, ma'am.
GOWDATHI.   There's nothing else to be done, is there?
BASSI.   No, ma'am.
GOWDATHI.   Give him to me, then.

The three of them start singing again. Gowdathi cooks
Jokumaraswami accordingly.

BASSI, SHARI   With a golden knife, on a diamond board
AND NINGI.   How shall I cut the Lord—
                Into pieces long or pieces broad ?
                I have cut the Lord.
                In a golden pot, on a diamond stove
                I put the Lord to boil,
                I boiled and cooked the dish
                And of the Lord I made a curry.
                Come, my taster, sweet taster,
                I wait with the food.
                That all-high God Jokumaraswami
                Do we worship.

GOWDATHI.   Bassi, see if Gowda has come.
BASSI *(looks outside and comes back).* Someone seems to be coming
                this way. It could be Gowda.
SHIVI.   I'll be going now, ma'am.
NINGI.   Me too, ma'am.
GOWDATHI.   Sit down, you can eat here and go later.
SHIVI.   No, ma'am, the children are waiting. They'll be hungry.

Shivi and Ningi leave. 'One' of Gowda's four servants enters.

ONE.	Madam . . .
GOWDATHI.	Hasn't Gowda come?
ONE.	No, madam.
GOWDATHI.	Where has he gone?
ONE.	He's gone to sleep in the field.
GOWDATHI.	To the field?
ONE.	That devil's field . . .
GOWDATHI.	Why did he go there today of all days?
ONE.	He's gone to sleep in the field to assert his ownership. He fought with Basanna, and has gone there saying, 'The field is mine, I'll sleep there.' He asked me to fetch him a blanket and some food.
GOWDATHI.	Just my luck! Take the blanket.
ONE.	He also asked for food.
GOWDATHI.	Take the blanket and go.

She gives him a blanket. The man takes it and leaves.

BASSI.	Go to bed now, ma'am. All that we've been doing since dawn has been wasted.
GOWDATHI.	You go and sleep. Why should you suffer because of me?
BASSI.	Then what will you do?
GOWDATHI.	What else can I do ? I'll fold my arms across my chest, and lie down, counting the beams on the ceiling.
BASSI.	Why can't Gowda understand?
GOWDATHI *(weeping, day dreaming).*	How else can I tell Gowda that I am a woman? A bird comes flying from afar and sits in its cage! It sings so that the earth itself becomes all ears and then a face, and arms and legs appear. The green breaks out and spreads. *(Sighs.)* That demon behind the moon won't let go. He catches the singing bird and all that green and the flowers and shoots are no more. Once more the same barren earth, the same gaunt, leafless trees, the same empty birds' nests. . .

(Meanwhile Bassi has left. Gowdathi sings softly.)

Bird of distant lands, come back to your nest.
That nest swings vacant in the breeze.

Storm wind that storms,
Whirlwind that whirls,
Slip through them, my bird,
Come to me, come to me.
The watchful eyes of old Satan—
Slip past them, my bird,
Come to me, come to me.
Exhilaration hides in every branch—
Make it sprout, my bird,
Come to me, come to me.
Sing the song of that land
Till the earth is all ears
And till the green spreads again.
Come my bird, come to me,
Come to me.

She suddenly remembers something and gets up. She packs the food, takes a container of water, places it on her head and goes out. Music.

The Bird Is Caught

A hut and a plant indicate a field. Gowda's four servants enter with the gun.

ONE.	Hasn't the sheep arrived yet?
TWO.	How can it? Who will come here knowingly to die?
THREE.	I'm hungry, why didn't you bring food?
ONE.	Gowdathi didn't give me food. She gave me the blanket, so I brought that.
FOUR.	So we will have to starve here until morning.
ONE.	Why until morning? Basanna will be here soon.
TWO.	Do you think he'll come?
FOUR.	We'll wait for about an hour or two.
THREE.	If he comes after we leave?
ONE.	He's not a coward, he will definitely come.
TWO.	Not long ago we killed his father. And today we have to kill the son— it's a grave sin.
FOUR.	Why should we bother about right and wrong?

TWO.	Actually, Basanna is not at fault.
THREE.	Doesn't he deny that the field was mortgaged?
TWO.	You know how our Gowda has swallowed fields belonging to various people. And still you can say Basanna is wrong!
ONE.	Why should we bother about all that? We'll do whatever we're asked to do. When we entered Gowda's employment, we swore before Hanuman that we would always be loyal to him, don't you remember?
TWO.	That's right.

Basanna springs on them suddenly. Before anyone can do anything, he grabs the gun. They scatter, frightened.

BASANNA *(brandishing the gun)*.	Do you know our god's name ? Dum Dum god. Here's a trigger. Behind that a bolt. You know what happens when this god says 'Dum' to people in front of him . . . they litter. You bastards, tell me where Gowda is.
ONE *(scared)*.	In Shari's house.
BASANNA.	He sent you here to finish me off, didn't he?
ONE.	Basanna . . .
BASANNA.	The devil killed my father here, didn't it?
ONE.	Basanna, please don't kill us, we beg you.
TWO.	Basanna, please forgive us. We'll do whatever you say.
BASANNA.	You'll do whatever I say?
TWO.	Yes.
BASANNA.	Then will you drag your arses and tell Gowda that you won't work for him any more?
ONE.	Will you give us back the gun?
BASANNA.	You want the gun ? *(He takes aim.)*
ALL FOUR.	Don't, please don't.
BASANNA.	Huh! Scram then. If you show your faces just once more, I'll kill you.

All go, dragging their arses. Basanna paces about for some time, takes the blanket left by them and goes to sleep in the hut. Gowdathi enters with food a little later.

GOWDATHI.	Couldn't you have come home yourself for a minute instead of sending a servant? You fought with Basanna and came here. Couldn't you have fought tomorrow? I

repeatedly told you so many times to come home for
dinner today. Get up, eat your food, get up! *(She serves
food in the dim light of the hut. Basanna eats silently.)*
There's such beautiful moonlight outside, why don't
you come out and eat? Gowda, how can I tell you my
joy? Look at our moon, Gowda, how big he is risen.
Something calls like a parrot. What's that bird? Why
don't you talk? You're angry with me, aren't you, for
having come out alone? Gowda, how can I tell you my
agony? You are, after all, a man and you don't need
children or a home. You feel you can go on like a lone
owl. I am a woman. How can I live without children?
Basanna has a parrot, Bassi told me. But can another's
parrot be ours? I am beginning to see our parrot in front
of me . . . Haven't you finished eating yet?

*Basanna tugs at her sari. Gowdathi runs out happily. As the song
is sung she tries to avoid him.*

BASANNA. How lovely! You've come out after ages like the rising
full moon. You come, your light like a lamp of eyes lit
up.
Your arms and thighs smooth like young banana stems
And lemons on your chest—
You, a bit of Paradise!
What a girl, what a complexion,
And what a slender waist,
Your eyes like mango slices—
Clap hand on hand
And come sit with me.

GOWDATHI. Young man! Do you know who you are talking to? You
are talking to the village's Gowdathi, a respectably
married woman. Are you aware of that? Tell me where
Gowda is.

BASANNA. So you want only your brave Gowda? You should've
gone to whore Shari's place, he's hanging around there.

GOWDATHI. How did this blanket come to be with you?

BASANNA. He sent four dogs here to get me killed like my father.
All of them got scared and left the blanket and gun here
and ran away.

GOWDATHI. Who are you, you rascal? What's your name? Your

caste?

BASANNA *(laughing).* Shall I say it in prose or verse?

GOWDATHI *(stamping her foot).* Stop grinning. Give up all hopes of
living and sing the song to my foot.

BASANNA.   Jingling your anklets,
Thrusting out your breasts,
You want to know my name.
My name, my name,
Write it down in your breast.
The lips of all the girls
Have only my name on them,
The girls call me,
Come, uncle Basanna.
The tongues of all the wives
Have only my name on them.
Their whispers say,
Come for a moment, Basanna, our king.
The mouths of all the hags
Have only my name on them,
They stammer, they stutter
Come, Jokumara.
Did you understand what I said, girl? All the girls in the
village know my name, Basanna. The women know, the
old, old hags know. Don't pretend you don't know me.
I'm asking you from the bottom of my heart, don't say
no. Come into the hut and let's talk for a while.

GOWDATHI.   Who's this shameless boy— lacking
Rhythm in his mouth,
Food to eat he has not,
And yet he stands slavering before me
And wants to lick.
A chaste wife am I.
Dare you attack me?
Rinse your mouth before you speak
Or your hair I'll pull out.
Gowdas we are of this place
And my man a brave knight—
Me you'd better not pursue
Or he'll oust and kill you.

BASANNA.   Ohohoho! Are you talking about your brave husband?

Are you talking about your valiant husband? Who is
your husband? The one who lays every girl in the
village and runs away just to show that he too is a man,
is he your husband? On the day when whores' seals have
to be broken, he snores under a blanket. Is he your brave
man? His wife has been panting for a talking parrot for
ten years and he couldn't get it— is he your husband?
What kind of a life is that?
You're suffering under an illusion.
Don't refuse, laughing.
My life you hold,
And fondle in your palm,
Don't make excuses
For refusing my friendship.

GOWDATHI.   Basanna, why commit this sin knowingly? Listen to
what I tell you.

BASANNA.   Go ahead, girl, tell me prettily.

GOWDATHI.   I am another's wife.
Don't pursue me, Basanna.
Remember what happened to Ravana?
You laugh, you come running,
You ogle, with hands outstretched.
Know, you imbecile, proper behaviour.
I am a married woman.
You dare not risk my enmity,
Know, you rascal, of right and wrong.

BASANNA.   There's no right or wrong
after eating Jokumaraswami curry.
Don't tell me.
Don't show me the bundle of scriptures.
I've read many books and
All of them say
That a man and woman should unite.
Girl, did you understand what I have been saying? Where
is the question of right and wrong after eating
Jokumaraswami curry? You came and fed me
Jokumaraswami, do you think I'll let you go now?
Only after I ate what you fed me did I start wanting you.
You ignore the one who has a talking parrot and search
for it elsewhere. How do you expect to find it? Come,

be friends with me, ask me for whatever bird you want.
Why don't you see, you hot, well-fed wench?
I implore, I'm at your feet,
Come to me, come to me.
I shall give you a bird that flies,
A lovely parrot that talks,
I shall adorn your hair with flowers, girl,
I implore, I'm at your feet,
Come to me, come to me.
Look at the full moon,
Listen to the birds sing,
Stop resisting!
The eastern wind sweeps, girl.
I implore, I'm at your feet,
Come to me, come to me.
Do you understand, girl? For ten years you've yearned
for a bird, and when the bird flies onto your lap you say
you don't want it. How can you do that?

GOWDATHI.   What shall I do? A singing parrot on one side, a
husband with daggers in his eyes on the other. Basanna,
why do you want to die needlessly? Just make way for
me.

BASANNA.   All this happened only after I ate what was put before
me. Go if you want to, I won't stop you. I'm not the
kind to lay an unwilling woman. As you go, drop by
Shari's house on the way; you can pick up Gowda there.

GOWDATHI.   He said he would be going to the field to sleep and he
has gone there.

BASANNA.   Here's another bit of news. Gowda now wants
Gurupada's daughter Ningi.

GOWDATHI.   What!

BASANNA.   Ask Shari.

A parrot screeches.

GOWDATHI.   Isn't that a bird screeching in the hut?

BASANNA.   Oh that? My talking parrot. Who knows, the cage
might have fallen down, or maybe it saw a snake.

GOWDATHI.   Quickly go and see what has happened.

BASANNA.   What's the use of having the parrot if you don't want it?

GOWDATHI.   When did I say I didn't want it ?

BASANNA.   Come, then.

Basanna gets the cage from inside the hut. Gowdathi is excited at seeing it.

GOWDATHI.   Nothing's wrong I hope?
BASANNA.   No.
GOWDATHI.   Does it talk?
BASANNA.   You haven't heard it speak yet. All the girls in the village are amazed at hearing it talk. It tells such wonderful stories.
GOWDATHI.   I want to hear this parrot talk and tell stories. Basanna, Basanna . . .
                  Inside the hut,
                  My beloved,
                  Let's go
                  Let's talk to the bird.
                  The eastern wind sweeps,
                  The flowers and trees bloom,
                  The bird's song is heard—
                  Let's talk to the bird.

The Defeat of Dum Dum God

MELA.   The Gowda wanders about
              Day and night
              And calls it 'love'—
              Chasing a chick,
              Chasing Ningi.
              Three months he's been wandering
              Like a cockerel
              Crowing each dawn,
              Deserting his field, his home,
              Shameless.
              But the chick has flown into Gurya's basket.

As the song is being sung, we see Gowda grabbing at Ningi, running behind her as she escapes, and so on.

GOWDA.   You have been eluding me for three months. The day I

What shall I do!
The Gowda comes to slay you!

(A scream is heard from afar.)

Basanna, open your eyes and see! They're not fireflies!
They are murderers. There are five hundred against one.
What can you do alone?

BASANNA.	You're right. Look, no torches can be seen in this direction. Run.
GOWDATHI.	How can I leave you alone and go?
BASANNA.	I'll definitely join the talking parrot wherever it is. Run away.
GOWDATHI.	If we have to run we'll go together. Or else let me die with you.
BASANNA.	The parrot's life is more precious than our lives. Run and save the parrot's life, don't stand here arguing uselessly. You will find me wherever the parrot is.
GOWDATHI.	You ask me to run?
BASANNA.	Quickly.
GOWDATHI.	You ?
BASANNA.	There you go again!
GOWDATHI.	Shall I run?
BASANNA.	Run, quickly. *(Gowdathi runs. Basanna stands looking after her.* The crazy girl has forgotten about me in her tummy. *(He looks around and takes up a sickle hanging on a tree. Before he can attack them bravely, he is surrounded by people wielding sickles and torches. Gowda is seen with his gun. Although alarmed, Basanna speaks up courageously.)* What, Gowda, come to see the field?

Even as he is saying this a man hits him from behind at Gowda's signal. Basanna falls. They pick him up a like a log and scream and dance.

All.	Slay, slay the village rascal! Son of a whore Basanna, get up! Gowdathi is calling.
	Luring girls
	With a talking parrot,
	Claiming all the fields as his—
	Let's make mincemeat out of him

With one blow.
Let's feed him to the eagle,
Let him mingle with the slush.

As the song ends, Gowda throws Basanna onto the ground and shoots him with the gun. The stage hushes as Basanna screams 'Aaah' After some time Sutradhara's voice is heard in the silence.

SUTRADHARA. Count and they are five hundred.
Count and the hands are a thousand
Which grip, chop the tender god.
A thousand hands, in each hand
A sickle or an axe
Which slash to death the tender god.
Killed and thrown him,
They have slashed and thrown him
And the flowing blood
Fills the river and the pond.
Where the blood falls,
Springs the sprout and the shoot,
And all the earth is fresh, is green.

Let a good government rule us,
Let children play in all homes,
May he who sows own the field,
May the country be filled with wealth and grain.
Come, my little Lord,
Come, my pretty moon,
Come, Jokumaraswami!

Curtain.